Praise for *How to Overcome Worry*

In a world filled with so much stress, fear, violence, and uncertainty—is it really possible to be "anxious for nothing"? Dr. Neely tackles head-on why these words aren't meant for someone else or another "more peaceful" time. He shows through great stories and biblical insights how God's Word is exactly what you and I need to face up to worry and fear—today—and how you can even put an unshakable foundation under your life story, even in a world that's shaking apart. It's quick to read, filled with hope and "I get that" examples. You need this book, like I did, to move fear for all that "could happen" to our children and country and world back into God's hands and put peace back into our hearts, today.

JOHN TRENT, PhD
Gary D. Chapman Chair of Marriage and Family Ministry and Therapy, Moody Theological Seminary

Worry is a relentless adversary. Thank you Winfred Neely for giving us sage, transferable wisdom in overcoming worry. This book is a treasure. It is practical, engaging, and, most important, it is anchored in the truth of God's Word.

DR. CRAWFORD W. LORITTS, JR.
Author, Speaker, Radio Host
Senior Pastor, Fellowship Bible Church

Worry is endemic. Yes, we do have a lot of things to worry about in our world today. Neely, in his inimitable pastoral style, puts our hearts to rest as he points us to our God, our fortress, our solid rock. This work is biblically sound, theologically astute, practically helpful, and spiritually warm. Don't worry . . . read Neely!

ABRAHAM KURUVILLA, ThM, MD, PhD
Research Professor of Pastoral Ministries,
Dallas Theological Seminary

Worry is like a flea on the back of a dog—it's not welcome but it attaches itself to any willing carrier. We are all well practiced in worry. We are not well rehearsed in overcoming worry. Neely's book provides the biblical information and practical advice to experience the peace of God in these trying times. I commend it to you. Start reading and stop worrying.

J. Paul Nyquist, PhD
President of Moody Bible Institute

This book focuses on one of the most important biblical passages that deal with worry. Winfred Neely provides solid biblical insight, practical wisdom, and pastoral sensitivity as he explores and applies how believers can wrestle with and win over worry.

Scott M. Gibson, DPhil
Haddon W. Robinson Professor of Preaching and Ministry, Gordon-Conwell Theological Seminary

HOW TO OVERCOME WORRY

Experiencing the
Peace of God
in Every Situation

DR. WINFRED NEELY

MOODY PUBLISHERS

CHICAGO

Edited by Connor Sterchi
Interior design: Ragont Design
Cover design: Erik M. Peterson

Library of Congress Cataloging-in-Publication Data

Names: Neely, Winfred, author.
Title: How to overcome worry : experiencing the peace of God in every situation /
  Dr. Winfred Neely.
Description: Chicago : Moody Publishers, 2017.
Identifiers: LCCN 2016056892 (print) | LCCN 2017007847 (ebook) | ISBN 9780802415042 |
  ISBN 9780802495181
Subjects: LCSH: Worry—Religious aspects—Christianity. | Anxiety—Religious
  aspects—Christianity. | Peace of mind—Religious aspects—Christianity. |
  Bible. Philippians, IV, 6-7—Criticism, interpretation, etc.
Classification: LCC BV4908.5 .N44 2017 (print) | LCC BV4908.5 (ebook) | DDC
  248.8/6--dc23
LC record available at https://lccn.loc.gov/2016056892

We hope you enjoy this book from Moody Publishers. Our goal is to provide high-quality, thought-provoking books and products that connect truth to your real needs and challenges. For more information on other books and products written and produced from a biblical perspective, go to www.moodypublishers.com or write to:

Moody Publishers
820 N. LaSalle Boulevard
Chicago, IL 60610

1 3 5 7 9 10 8 6 4 2

Printed in the United States of America

I dedicate this book to Stephne Elaine Neely, my wife of forty years and my best friend. She is a woman of God, a wonderful mother, a mentor of women and men, and one of the most courageous women I know. I would not be the man I am today without her redemptive influence in my life! I am grateful to her for walking with me through the anxious moments and seasons of the last four decades.

Contents

1

The Troubled Waters of Worry

They reeled and staggered like a drunken man, and were at their wits' end. Then they cried to the LORD in their trouble, and He brought them out of their distresses. He caused the storm to be still, so that the waves of the sea were hushed.

PSALM 107:27-29

I can remember a scene from my youth: My mother is the center of attention, sitting at our kitchen table with her head slightly bowed. I am standing at the head of the table, listening to her. I cannot recall the circumstances or the problem, but I still remember my mother's words: "I am worried." The tone of her voice, the deep lines in her face, and the slump in her shoulders all testified to the depth of her anxiety.

Something was bothering her. And I didn't like it! It didn't seem fair to me that she should have to encounter the troubled waters of worry. After all, she held my childhood universe together. She was radiant with compassion, kindness, and consideration for others. Against the background of her caring nature, emotional stability, and winsome personality, these symptoms of excess worry stood out in bold relief.

Through the years, I have had a number of lightbulb moments when I moved from ignorance to insight about some aspect of the human condition. Here is one: During my teenage years, between the ages of thirteen and eighteen, when my grandmother didn't think I would live to be twenty-five, I was responsible for many of the worrisome circumstances and anxious days in my mother's life. I cringe in shame as I reflect on some of the stupid and destructive decisions I made.

If I remember correctly, it started on the day I graduated from the eighth grade. Proud of me, my mother gave me permission to get on the bus with a group of friends from the neighborhood and go across the city to Go Kart Land, an amusement park. She also gave me strict instructions to be home by ten o'clock that night.

I bolted out of the house, ran down the stairs, and caught up with my friends. When we arrived at Go Kart Land, we descended from the bus, breathing anticipation and excitement. That day we quenched our thirst for adolescent freedom on the go-karts. But for some reason, I decided to ignore the perfectly reasonable curfew given to me by my mother. I *deliberately* lost track of the time.

In the meantime, on the other side of the city, my mother did not know why I was late or where I was. As she said later, "I didn't know if you were sick, dead, or dying." We did not have smartphones in 1968, but if we had, I doubt I would have called home or answered her call. It would not even have occurred to me to send her a text message explaining my tardiness. Nor did it occur to my adolescent mind to step into a nearby phone booth, place a coin in the slot, call home, and ease my mother's concern.

It was way past ten o'clock when I got home that night. Mother was worried about what had happened to me; I was worried about what she was going to do to me when she saw me! I tiptoed up our back stairs, opened the door quietly, and tried to sneak into the house, to no avail. My father was asleep, but my mother was still up!

I can still see her, stepping around the corner, her eyes filled with a mingling of love and maternal fury. She confronted me in the kitchen with the words, "Boy, why are you so late?" She was relieved when she saw me, but gave me a piece of her mind.

Some years later, she remarked to me that on that night, she had offered a prayer of intercession: "Lord, just bring Winfred home, and then I will kill him!" She had no intention of taking my life, of course, but her prayer expressed the depth of her anxiety.

THE DEEPS OF WORRY

I did not understand then, but I understood later. When the ship of my life sailed out of the river of singlehood into the ocean of adulthood, marriage, and fatherhood, I felt for the first time the powerful, deep, and overwhelming currents of anxiety over my children. I had never felt such currents before. The experience was new and troubling, but it would have been irresponsible to retreat to the safety of the river. I remembered these words:

Those who go down to the sea in ships,
Who do business on great waters;
They have seen the works of the LORD,
And His wonders in the deep.
For He spoke and raised up a stormy wind,
Which lifted up the waves of the sea.
They rose up to the heavens, they went down to the
    depths;
Their soul melted away in their misery,
They reeled and staggered like a drunken man,
And were at their wits' end. (Ps. 107:23–27)

The ocean is where God wanted me to be, but the stormy winds have often "lifted up the waves," causing my wife and me to be at wits' end with anxiety over one of our precious children.

Our son Sterling was born in Senegal, West Africa, the country where Stephne and I served as missionaries for nearly a decade. During those years, we evangelized the lost, nurtured and equipped believers, worked in prison ministry, and started a training institution for pastors, evangelists, and laypeople. We developed deep relationships that we enjoy to this day.

> The theological wrestling match deepened our anxiety as we struggled with questions about the sovereign care of God.

As much as we love Senegal and its people, I must admit that the environment and climate are not always conducive to health. During the rainy season, the temperature can soar to 120 degrees, with almost suffocating humidity. Malaria in Senegal is as frequent as the common cold in North America. At different times, every member of our family had malaria.

On one occasion, we thought that Sterling had contracted malaria again. My wife noticed it first. Sterling was lethargic. He had diarrhea and a fever. At that point in our missionary career, we were no longer troubled about malaria and knew how to treat it. Thinking that Sterling had malaria, we gave him the needed meds. But he did not improve, and our anxiety increased.

We decided to take Sterling to a competent and well-respected pediatrician in Dakar. We were shocked when the doctor proceeded to treat Sterling for typhoid fever. He was just a little boy. Stephne and I were living out

God's call on our lives. Couldn't our great and infinite Father protect our little guy from a sickness like typhoid fever? The theological wrestling match deepened our anxiety as we struggled with questions about the sovereign care of God. My personal worries deepened as I entertained other questions: Lord, did I do something to displease You? Are You trying to get my attention by allowing Sterling to get sick? Is this a test?

> Sometimes His ways are shrouded in mystery, and we struggle to make sense of pain, tragedy, and the unexpected.

Our observations of God's ways with other godly missionaries did not help. We knew one missionary couple with three wonderful children. One day the husband was out jogging in a park in Dakar with his son, when suddenly the father collapsed in front of his son and died of a massive heart attack. He was just thirty-nine years old. After burying her husband, the widow returned to Senegal with her children to serve Christ. About a year after her husband's death, one of her sons was hit by a car and killed. A family of five was now reduced to a family of three. I feel a strange numbness as I recount this event. Stephne and I knew another missionary couple who had one little boy, and their baby boy died at the tender age of eight months.

In light of these stories, was my little boy, now being treated for typhoid fever, going to be next?

I am not questioning God's wisdom and goodness in these circumstances, but what I am saying is that sometimes His ways are shrouded in mystery, and we struggle to make sense of pain, tragedy, and the unexpected. God generally does not explain Himself to us in those times. Rather, He tells us who He is! He reminds us that He is good, He is wise, He is faithful, He is in control. Stephne and I had to step out and entrust our little boy to God. Our concern was sharp, but this attitude eased our anxiety. We cried to the Lord in our worry, and "He caused the storm to be still, so that the waves of the sea were hushed" (Ps. 107:29).

The Lord brought Sterling through his illness, and we were thankful. Still, I must admit that even in our capacity as full-time Christian workers, missionaries, and parents, we were worried.

OUR ANXIOUS NEW WORLD

After forty years of marriage, thirty-one years of full-time Christian ministry, and six decades of living, one of my big takeaways is that we live in a worry-filled and anxiety-driven world. Every day it seems new anxiety-creating circumstances intrude on our lives.

In the twenty-first century, these threats seem larger, more frequent, and more menacing. Terrorism, economic uncertainty, the recent resurgence of racial unrest, the murder of respected police officers in the line of duty, the murder of unarmed civilians by rogue cops, the breakdown of trust between law enforcement and the citizenry, senseless gun violence, the danger some children face as they walk to and from school, mass shootings of innocent people, the moral and spiritual crisis of the Western world, and the erosion and blatant rejection of traditional values—all of these realities generate worry in many of us. Gary Collins puts it this way:

Chaotic overscheduling, worry over tests, the disappearance of family routines or stability, endless exposure to disturbing information, lack of close connections, constant change, insecurity, information overload, pressures from peers, and the fading of clear moral guidelines all combine to raise anxiety levels in young people. . . . Constant reminders about the ongoing activity of terrorists around the world have heightened our insecurities and led to what has been called "the new anxiety."[1]

In 2012, a man dressed in tactical clothing opened fire inside a movie theater in Colorado. Since then, a number of shootings have occurred inside theaters, producing a dark cloud of anxiety on what was once considered a worry-free pastime.

My wife and I are avid moviegoers, and we recently went to see a newly released blockbuster. As the lights dimmed, and I prepared to listen to the instruction from the big screen about how cellphone usage during the film spoils the experience for others, I heard this new, troubling warning: "Let's talk safety. If you see any strange people or strange activity, let someone from our staff know." I settled into my seat in the theater, but I paid close attention to people when they left or came in.

Since September 11, 2001, bold signs hang on the walls of trains that read: "If you see something, say something." The exhortation itself heightens our sense that danger may be lurking in the shadows. In a world where terrorist attacks are a reality, the signage on train walls can generate a new low-grade anxiety.

We live in a world of global communications with a never-ending, 24/7 news cycle. We watched in real time as the terrorist attacks in Paris unfolded. We have repeatedly watched the news in horror as ISIS fanatics behead their captives. It is not an overstatement to say that our entire planet is worried.

Even church sanctuaries are not necessarily safe havens. The church bombing in Birmingham in 1963 showed that not even churches are off limits. And more recent events like the shooting that occurred in a Charleston church's prayer meeting and threats against pastors who preach the gospel have raised new concerns about security during church services.

Mass shootings in schools, universities, theaters, and

churches have demolished our naïve assumptions about the safety and security of these places. Respect and honor resulting in sensible behavior is no longer a given in these traditional havens of rest. The twenty-first century is a new, high-tech world full of anxiety and worry, yet our old anxieties have not left us.

You may be a part of the sandwich generation, with children at home on the one hand and aging parents for whom you are responsible on the other. You never dreamed life would be this hard and demanding. You are worried about your capacity to continue at this pace.

> Anxiety can reside in virtually every nook and cranny of human experience. Its causes are myriad, and it is no respecter of persons or circumstances.

You may be a mother with a tendency to worry. Perhaps you have a son or a daughter who is struggling, or maybe your new baby is ill. You may even feel guilty because you are so utterly helpless in the face of your child's overwhelming need. You are worried, preoccupied with the pressures of life, feeling like you are all alone.

You may be a grandparent, enjoying your golden years, when out of the blue, and for reasons beyond your control, you find yourself caring for your grandchildren. You love these kids, but you are tired all the time. You worry that you have to bear these burdens alone.

Your spouse may be a police officer. You have a good marriage, and although the safety of police officers has always been a concern, it is a major concern today. And, if you are honest, you are no longer just a concerned husband or wife; you are downright worried.

You may be single, and while there isn't anything wrong with singleness, you want to get married one day, have a life partner, someone you can grow old with. You have laid out your biblical criteria for a spouse in the presence of God, but weeks, months, and years have gone by, and you are still single. And the desire to be married is no longer simply a concern but a preoccupation.

THE THEOLOGICAL, EXISTENTIAL, AND PRACTICAL QUESTION

Even though worry has taken on new forms and descended with a vengeance on former havens of tranquility, it is a problem as old as the ancient text of Scripture. Our struggle with worry is a part of the human condition. Anxiety can reside in virtually every nook and cranny of human experience. Its causes are myriad, and it is no respecter of persons or circumstances. And Christians are not exempt!

In light of such a reality, the theological, existential, and practical questions that we as Christians must address are: How do we overcome anxiety in a worry-filled world? How do we obtain victory over worry in situations that are charged with anxiety? When a raging sea of anxiety rises up in our souls, how do we keep ourselves from drowning?

The purpose of this book is to answer this question biblically. May we all embrace heaven's answer.

2

A Bold Imperative

Be anxious for nothing.
PHILIPPIANS 4:6A

Paul was a living embodiment of *divine* power and *human* cooperation in the conquest of anxiety. When we read through Paul's letter to the Philippians, which is both a friendship letter and thank-you note, we meet in Paul a man full of divine joy (1:4, 18, 25), gratitude (4:18), and concern for others (2:19–23). His passion for Christ strikes us with compelling force. In an outburst of passion, he declares that the Lord Jesus is his reason for living (1:21), the ultimate example of an attitude of giving, service, and humility (2:5–11), the object of his ardent pursuit (3:7–14), and his strength in all things (4:13).

But when Paul, under the Holy Spirit's guidance and power, penned the words, "Be anxious for nothing," he was facing extremely dire circumstances. For the cause of Christ, the noblest reason on earth, he was in prison! And even though the cause of his imprisonment was noble (1:13) and God used his imprisonment to promote the gospel (1:12) and even lead some of Caesar's own household to Christ (4:22), humanly speaking, Paul had every reason to worry and be preoccupied with his incarceration.

> Many of us have already tried to turn off the water faucet of anxiety but have not been able to do so. That's because the ability to do this is grace-enabled, faith-based, and Spirit-empowered.

To make matters worse, Nero was the emperor of Rome at the time. Nero was a cruel and sadistic ruler. In fact, he had his own mother and his wife murdered. (Nero did not want to share power with anyone, including his mother, so he ordered her to be hunted down and murdered, and Nero himself killed his second wife after she had chided him for coming home late from one of the gladiatorial games.)

Obviously, Paul had every reason to worry about the result of standing before Nero for justice!

But he was not overcome by worry. Without a doubt, Paul, being a man of like passions with us, experienced anxiety about his circumstances. But he had learned how to walk in victory. We can and must learn this liberating lesson as well.

We overcome worry by ceasing to give in to worry. We conquer anxiety by turning off the water faucet of anxiety in our own souls.

Now you may be thinking, *Here we go again. Another unrealistic approach to handling life's problems. If I could just turn off my anxiety like a faucet, I would not be reading this book!*

Paul, however, is not calling for mere human effort in these verses. Many of us have already tried to turn off the water faucet of anxiety but have not been able to do so. That's because the ability to do this is grace-enabled, faith-based, and Spirit-empowered. By faith we yield our hearts and minds and will to God (Rom. 6:12–14; 12:1–2), and then the Holy Spirit fills us (Eph. 5:18) and empowers us (Rom. 15:13) as we cooperate with the Lord in the process of resisting anxiety. In this process of sanctification, turning off the water faucet of worry is the first step toward victory.

HEALTHY CONCERN AND CARE

The Greek verb *μεριμνάω* or *merimnao*—translated "be anxious" in Philippians 4:6a—and its cognates are used in two important ways in Scripture. First, they are used to indicate healthy *concern* and care. For example, in Philippians 2:20 the verb is translated as *concerned*. Paul says to Timothy, "I have no one else of kindred spirit who will genuinely be *concerned* for your welfare" (emphasis added). In 1 Corinthians 12:25, the verb is translated as *care* when Paul says, "So that there may be no division in the body, but that the members may have the same *care* for one another."

Genuine concern and care for others is biblical (see 1 Cor. 7:32–35; 12:25; 2 Cor. 11:28). Concern in this sense is the attitude of the heart leading to practical expressions of care for the well-being of another. Concern is a mark of healthy mutual relationships (1 Cor. 7:33–34), a character trait of the godly servant of Christ (2 Cor. 11:28), and should be one of the hallmarks of the interpersonal dynamics of local church life (1 Cor. 12:22–26). Healthy husbands and wives are concerned for one another and their families. Healthy followers of Christ exhibit biblical concern when they share in the sorrows and joys of others.

So the call to turn off the water faucet of worry is not a call to indifference, nor is it an excuse to be irresponsible and unconcerned about people, problems, and life. If your child is ill, you don't have to worry, but you should be concerned. If you are struggling with finances, you don't have to worry, but you should be concerned. We should care!

I am reminded of this each time I look at the quote hanging on the wall in my apartment kitchen: "Unless someone like you cares a whole awful lot, nothing is going to get better. It's not."[1]

> Worry is concern turned inward and deformed, divorced from the grace of God and rooted in unhealthy fear.

Second, the above Greek verbs are also translated *anxiety* or *worry* (see Matt. 6:25–34; 10:19; 13:22; Luke

10:41; 21:34; 1 Peter 5:7). For instance, in Luke 10:38–42 we read a short narrative about household stress, during which Jesus subverts our expectations by issuing a mild rebuke to Martha. Calling her by name twice, the Lord tenderly points out the heart of her (and our) problem. I imagine Jesus looking at Martha with grace in His eyes and compassion in His voice as He says to her, "Martha, Martha, you are *worried* and bothered about *so many things*" (Luke 10:41, emphasis added).

In the Sermon on the Mount, the Lord Jesus devoted an entire movement to talk to us about worry and anxiety. With the authority of heaven, Jesus the King commands us:

> "That is why I tell you not to worry about everyday life—whether you have enough food and drink, or enough clothes to wear. Isn't life more than food, and your body more than clothing? Look at the birds. They don't plant or harvest or store food in barns, for your heavenly Father feeds them. And aren't you far more valuable to him than they are? Can all your worries add a single moment to your life?" (Matt. 6:25–27 NLT)

While under house arrest in Rome, Paul took the time to compose a letter and, echoing the Master, he says the same thing to the Philippians and to us, "Be anxious for nothing."

DEFINING ANXIETY

Now that we have distinguished the translation and usage of the same terms in different contexts, it's time to define *anxiety* as it is used in Scripture. I consider *anxiety* and *worry* to be interchangeable. My definition is not intended to reflect a therapeutic or psychological approach but rather is based on a study of the negative use of the terms in Scripture. I recognize that some people have clinical anxiety as a medical condition. Anxiety is one of many evidences that we live in a fallen world. There are complex factors that may contribute to it, but in this book, I am concerned with anxiety as worry rooted in unbelief.

In the New Testament, *worry* is the sinful response of the human heart and mind to real difficulties and problems in life. The problems and circumstances that elicit anxiety and worry are not imaginary. Worry is concern turned inward and deformed, divorced from the grace of God and rooted in unhealthy fear. In addition, it is a practical expression of unbelief, causing a distraction from what is essential in life and resulting in misplaced priorities. This is what it means to be anxious in the biblical sense of the term.

Of course, Christians still struggle with anxiety, but habitual worry is a trait of someone who is not in an intimate relationship with God (Matt. 6:31–32). Jesus asserted that anxiety has the potential to silence the power of God's Word in a person's life (Matt. 13:22).

When understood in this scriptural way, the believer's failure to conquer anxiety is more serious than it appears. That's not to say that a Christian struggling with anxiety is not a genuine believer, but that we need to take seriously the scriptural challenge to "be anxious for nothing."

In his book *Christian Counseling*, Gary Collins explains how worry is generated:

> Worry comes when we *turn from God, shift* the burdens of life on to ourselves and *assume*, at least by our *attitude* and actions, that we alone are responsible for handling problems. *Instead*

of acknowledging God's sovereignty and power, or seeking His kingdom and righteousness first, many of us . . . *slip* into sinful self-reliance and preoccupation with our own life pressures.[2] (emphasis added)

Collins's elaboration on the process of anxiety is helpful because it clarifies for us what is involved in the command to not worry. In giving us the imperative, "Be anxious for nothing," God is commanding us to look *to* Him instead of turning *from* Him. He is commanding us to shift our burdens onto Him instead of placing them on our own shoulders. He is commanding us to assume by our attitudes and actions that we are not solely responsible for handling life's problems.

Instead of slipping into sinful self-reliance and preoccupation with the pressures of life, we are to acknowledge God's sovereignty and power, and seek His kingdom and righteousness first. It is also important to consider the cultural context of Philippians 4:6–7, which runs counter to our Western individualistic mindset. In the United States, individualism may be a cultural cataract that prevents us from seeing the corporate implications of church life. Most of the imperatives in the New Testament are given to the community and not to the individual. The verb used in this sentence ("Be anxious for nothing") is second person plural, so the commandment is actually given to the Philippian church as a whole. Paul is saying, "All of y'all stop worrying." This is God's call to every local community of Christ followers on the planet! What if the local church as a whole embraced this call to conquer anxiety, joining together and looking to the Lord instead of being driven by worry?

ANXIETY IS A CHOICE

The verbal construction of "be anxious for nothing" is also important because it calls us to *stop* an action that is already in progress. Anxiety is being presented not only as a noun, but as a verb. Understood biblically, therefore, anxiety is also a choice and an action that can be stopped. The Philippian church was a model church in the sense that they loved the Lord and they supported Paul's ministry, yet they were collectively engaged in the ongoing action of worry. In effect, God said to the Philippian church, "Stop worrying. Stop it today. Stop it now."

One of the lessons we learn from the Philippians is that mature followers of Christ can and do experience worry individually and also collectively as married couples, as families, and as a church. But even though worry may already be entrenched in your life, God has the holy audacity to say, "Be anxious for nothing."

This is a bold imperative. *Nothing* means nothing. Ponder the comprehensive nature of this commandment. There isn't *anything* in life that should cause us to slip into the pit of sinful self-reliance. In a very real sense, this commandment should give birth to praise; it demands a heartfelt hallelujah. We should breathe a sigh of relief at the good news implied in the imperative.

For many parents, there is the frequent temptation to move beyond concern to worry. For singles, the worry of not finding a godly spouse can become a fixation. For those with a spouse in law enforcement, the grip of anxiety can be suffocating.

Again, we can be concerned. But we don't have to be worried.

Remember, we overcome worry by ceasing to give in to worry. By God's grace and enablement, we conquer anxiety by turning off the faucet of anxiety in our own souls. But then what?

Then, we pray, taking any worries, anxieties, troubles, and concerns to our caring heavenly Father.

3

The Antidote
to Worry

*But in everything by prayer and supplication with
thanksgiving let your requests be made known to God.*

PHILIPPIANS 4:6B

So is there any specific instruction from the Lord to
those of us who are anxious? Yes! Paul tells us in the
second part of Philippians 4:6 to take everything to the
Lord in prayer. The next (and vital) step to overcoming
worry is to pray. Pray about everything.

*We conquer worry by taking everything to the Lord
in prayer.*

The second part of verse 6 begins with the conjunction *but*, which in the original Greek text is em-
phatic; it highlights the contrast between anxiety and

prayer. Prayer in everything is the antidote to worrying about anything.

In the phrase "but in everything," the little word *in* has great practical significance for us. As we journey through life toward heaven, we find ourselves *in* various circumstances and situations. The situations and contexts of our lives will shift, vary, and change.

"In everything" means in *every* situation, in *every* circumstance, in *every* problem. It's comprehensive, embracing life in all of its shifts and turns, highs and lows, and ups and downs!

We tend to live as if the situations in our lives are either too big or too trivial for God. Of course we may not admit it, but sometimes we act like our particular situation is too great for Him. If we had the resources, we would step in and resolve the problem ourselves. Or we bury our heads in the sand and try to ignore the harsh winds of difficulty blowing around us.

Alternatively, we may have the attitude that our

> Prayer in everything is the antidote to worrying about anything.

circumstances are too trivial for God's interest. Or we may be so confused, so conflicted in our emotions, and so exhausted by intense mental and spiritual battles that we forget that even in these circumstances, prayer is appropriate and necessary. For all practical purposes, we are declaring our situation to be outside the influence of our God.

A MOTHER'S INFLUENCE

The death of my mother was one such circumstance for me. It suddenly seemed as if the years had passed at the speed of light. Just a moment before, I had been a six-year-old boy watching my mother walking up the hall and saying kindly, "Winfred, I am going to teach you how to pray." After kneeling beside me, she had tenderly instructed me how to converse with God. Now I was a middle-aged husband and father of four children standing beside a hospital bed, along with sixteen other relatives and close friends, watching my mother live her last few minutes on earth. Actually, we did more than watch. We participated in a painful and yet strangely glorious event—the home-going of a follower of the Lord Jesus Christ.

But my mother's last years on earth were difficult. She

had been ill for some time. She had a major heart attack in 1984, underwent open-heart surgery in 1992, and suffered from diabetes and congestive heart failure. Since she was having a serious problem with lethal abnormal heart rhythms, her doctors decided to place an implantable defibrillator in her chest. She agreed to have the procedure done, hoping the device would greatly improve the quality of her life. When she had an abnormal heart rhythm, the defibrillator administered an electric shock, converting her abnormal heart rhythm back to a normal one.

My mother was devastated to discover that the implantable defibrillator would not and could not meet her expectations. The first time the defibrillator administered a shock to her heart, she was scared, and she cried out in pain from the shocks. From time to time, her defibrillator would jolt her heart muscle with an electric shock. This went on for about a year. She was in the midst of a painful and scary ordeal. Eventually, her heart gave out. During the last few days of her life, her defibrillator was shocking her heart muscle regularly, sometimes every few minutes.

When she was hospitalized, I was sitting in a doctoral seminar at Trinity Evangelical Divinity School. An administrator walked into the classroom and told me that I needed to go to the hospital immediately. When I arrived at Lutheran General Hospital in Park Ridge, Illinois, she was not doing well. As I sat talking to her, the defibrillator went off, and my precious mother grimaced in pain and arched her back because of the electric shock. Instinctively, we all wanted to touch and comfort her, but we could not for fear of being shocked ourselves. I stood there helpless, horrified, and stunned. My mother wanted the doctor to turn the defibrillator off; the frequency and intensity of the shocks were too much for her to bear. My siblings and I, in consultation with the doctors, decided to comply with her wishes.

When the doctor came into her room to turn off her defibrillator, he gently explained to her what he was doing. All sixteen of us stood around her bed and watched; it seemed as if we were standing on the edge of eternity. The nurse injected morphine into her IV line to ease the pain she would experience in a few minutes when the arrhythmias started. The doctor then left the room.

Uneasiness gripped me as we stood around my mother's bed. I wanted to say so many things to her but was unable. I knew she had only a few more minutes left on this side of heaven. Pain rose up in my chest. Suddenly my daughter Rachel started singing a hymn, and we all joined in. Then my daughter Eden prayed. Then others began speaking up, offering a spontaneous reading of appropriate Scripture verses, saying earnest prayers on my mother's behalf, and singing some of the great hymns and choruses of the faith.

Then it happened—I looked at my mother's heart monitor and saw that the lethal abnormal heart rhythm had started. All we could do was stand there and watch as it ran its awful course. I grabbed my Bible and read Psalm 23 aloud as my mother grimaced in pain. Then we continued to sing, pray, and read Scripture as my mother was being welcomed home to glory! The Holy Spirit filled that hospital room! God's presence was real, tangible, and comforting. In the midst of such pain and grief, we sensed God's glory and knew we were having a divine visitation. On her bed, my

> Prayer is conversation with God and is the means through which we draw on the resources of heaven for our pain and struggles here on earth.

mother slightly turned her head to the left as I watched. She was gone.

I shed tears as I write. The whole scene moved the nurse deeply. Aware that he had just witnessed something extraordinary, he said, "I have never seen anything like this in my entire life."

Our ability to pray and talk to God is one of the glories and privileges of being beside a saved loved one in their passing. Even in circumstances such as witnessing a loved one die, prayer is always appropriate, and it is a powerful testimony to the glory of God! Thanks be to God that we can talk with Him in a situation like this, and in fact in any situation or context, drawing strength and help, and harnessing heavenly resources through prayer.

A PRECIOUS PRIVILEGE

Prayer, then, in all of life, is one of the most effective, precious, life-transforming, and God-honoring means of grace that our heavenly Father has placed at our disposal. To be able to talk to our heavenly Father is one of the greatest privileges we have on earth! Prayer is conversation with God and is the means through which we draw on the resources of heaven for our pain and struggles here on earth.

In the Bible, prayer was one of the means through which God's people obtained grace, help, wisdom, and strength from God. Consider the anguished prayer of Hannah (1 Sam. 1:10–11), the desperate prayer of Hezekiah (Isa. 38:2–3), the defiant prayers of Daniel (Dan. 6:6–13), the moving laments and confessions of the Psalms (see Pss. 22; 51). Consider the prayers of God's people to come in the tribulation (Rev. 5:8; 6:9–10) as well as the vibrant prayers of God's people in the book of Acts (1:14; 2:42; 4:23–31; 12:1–17; 13:1–3). J. B. Phillips said this about the first-century believers in his 1955 preface to Acts in *The New Testament in Modern English*:

> It is impossible to spend several months in close study of the remarkable short book . . . without being profoundly stirred, and to be honest, disturbed. The reader is disturbed because he is seeing Christianity, *the real thing*, in action for the first time in human history. The newborn Church, as *vulnerable* as any human child, having

neither *money, influence* nor *power* in the ordinary sense, is setting forth *joyfully* and *courageously* to win the pagan world for Christ. Yet we cannot help feeling disturbed as well as moved, for this is surely the Church as it was meant to be. It is *vigorous* and *flexible.* ... These men did not "say their prayers," they really prayed. But if they were uncomplicated and naïve by modern standards, we have to admit that they were open on the Godward side in a way that is *almost unknown today.*[1] (emphasis added)

Prayer was one of the outstanding traits of our Lord's life and ministry on earth. In Luke's Gospel, the evangelist emphasizes His prayer life (see Luke 5:16; 6:12; 9:18; 23:34). Matthew and Mark narrate our Lord's baptism and transfiguration, but Luke alone tells us that He prayed on these occasions. Luke says this about Jesus' baptism:

Now when all the people were baptized, Jesus was also baptized, and while He was *praying,* heaven was opened, and the Holy Spirit descended upon Him in bodily form like a dove, and a voice came out of heaven, "You are My beloved Son, in You I am well-pleased." (Luke 3:21–22, emphasis added)

Luke then recounts the incredible moments of our Lord's transfiguration:

Some eight days after these sayings, He took along Peter and John and James, and went up on the mountain to *pray*. And while He was *praying*, the appearance of His face became different, and His clothing became white and gleaming. And behold, two men were talking with Him; and they were Moses and Elijah, who, appearing in glory, were speaking of His departure which He was about to accomplish at Jerusalem. (Luke 9:28–31, emphasis added)

The Lord's purpose in going up to the mountain was not to be transfigured but to pray, and while praying, He was transfigured. And who cannot be moved at the anguished prayer of the Lord Jesus in the garden of Gethsemane?

When He arrived at the place, He said to them, *"Pray that you may not enter into temptation."* And He withdrew from them about a stone's throw, and He knelt down and began to *pray*, saying, "Father, if You are willing, remove this cup from Me; yet not My will, but Yours be done." Now an angel from heaven appeared to Him, strengthening Him. And being in agony He was *praying* very fervently; and His sweat became like drops of blood, falling down upon the ground. When He rose from *prayer*, He came to the disciples and found them sleeping from sorrow, and said to them, "Why are you sleeping? Get up and *pray that you may not enter into temptation."* (Luke 22:40–46, emphasis added)

Prayer was a vital part of Jesus' life. Even on the cross while enveloped in supernatural darkness, before He bowed His sacred head, breathed His last, and voluntarily yielded up His spirit in death, prayer was on His sinless lips: "Father, into Your hands I commit My spirit" (Luke 23:46).

Our Lord demonstrated to us that no matter how

dark it gets, prayer is still appropriate and necessary. It is quite possible that in our digital, high-tech, and secular world, with all of its scientific advances, we may underestimate the place and power of prayer in our lives as followers of Christ. Today, if we have an epidemic, an economic crisis, or some major technological setback, as a culture, we call on technocrats, scientists, or other experts to solve the problems of the environment and the human condition. The big idea of twenty-first-century life is to work the problem until we find a solution. God is not even a part of the problem-solving equation. In the ancient world, people called on God or idols, but twenty-first-century secular culture and mindset does not consider prayer to be a major part of a solution on earth. And because we live in a culture with this worldview, this mindset can seep into us and shape how we think about prayer.

Sensing how the culture was shaping the thinking of the church in 1961, A. W. Tozer wrote:

> We are today suffering from a secularized mentality. Where the sacred writers saw God, we see laws of nature. Their world was fully populated;

ours is all but empty. Their world was alive and personal; ours is impersonal and dead. God ruled their world; ours is ruled by the laws of nature, and we are always once removed from the presence of God.[2]

In our world where people are once, twice, or perhaps three times removed from the presence of God through the so-called laws of nature, science, and digital technology, we may underestimate the place of prayer in our lives as Christians. But if we take the Bible seriously, it is clear that prayer should hold a big place in our lives today. It is key to the conquest of worry. This is why Paul is essentially saying in Philippians: but in everything by (the means of) prayer and (by the means of) supplication let your requests be known to God.

DIFFERENT KINDS OF PRAYER

Paul uses different terms for the different aspects of conversing with God: *prayer, supplication, thanksgiving*, and *requests*. The Greek word προσευχῇ that is translated *prayer* is the most general and the most frequently used term for prayer in the New Testament. Prayer can be both personal and corporate and is a real, genuine conversation with God, marked by reverence and a worshipful attitude, as well as submission and trust. But in order to understand this verse, we must also explore the different facets of prayer.

Supplication

Supplication is prayer that expresses our need before God. To be human is to be needy. We are finite and limited. We do not know everything, and we are not all-wise. All of us need the Lord. The only one who exists without need is God. But we need Him desperately! Supplication is the means by which we express our need of Him, and our need of His power, presence, and wisdom.

> We come to God, or we are driven to Him, forced to our knees by the burden of life's circumstances, and in desperation we cry out to Him, expressing our need.

In the movie *It's a Wonderful Life*, George Bailey becomes desperate when Uncle Billy misplaces a huge sum of the business's money. George is so worried that he begins to contemplate suicide. He makes his way to a restaurant and takes a seat at the bar. Lines of despair twist his face, his hair is uncombed, and he prays, "Dear Father in heaven, I'm not a praying man, but if you're up there and you can hear me, show me the way. I'm at the end of my rope. Show me the way, God."

We come to God, or we are driven to Him, forced to our knees by the burden of life's circumstances, and in desperation we cry out to Him, expressing our need. This is supplication.

Thanksgiving

Thanksgiving means gratitude. Thanksgiving is the grateful acknowledgment that God exists, that He is good, and that He is sovereign. It is the thankful recognition of God for everything He has done, is doing, and will do on our behalf.

Thanksgiving will last forever, carrying on into eternity (Rev. 4:9; 7:12; 11:17). We won't fully understand how much we owe God until we set foot on the shores

> In giving God thanks, we are already moving out of the dark forest of worry and into the meadow of peace.

of glory. But in the meantime, thankfulness should always accompany prayer and should be our posture in all life circumstances (Col. 3:17; 1 Thess. 5:18). In giving God thanks, we are already moving out of the dark forest of worry and into the meadow of peace.

Requests

Requests are specific needs or things we ask God to grant us. Our requests are specific and contextual, arising out of real needs with the expectation of receiving real and definite help from God. When we are in anxiety-inducing circumstances, we should figure out what we need and take those needs to God in prayer.

In the Bible, Daniel and his three friends were in danger of losing their lives. The king had determined to kill off the wise men of Babylon, including Daniel and his three friends. The situation was charged with anxiety. But what did Daniel and his friends do?

Then Daniel went to his house and informed his friends, Hananiah, Mishael and Azariah, about the matter, so that they might request compassion from the God of heaven concerning this mystery, so that Daniel and his friends would not be destroyed with the rest of the wise men of Babylon. (Dan. 2:17–18)

The Lord granted them their request, and the interpretation of the dream was revealed to Daniel. Daniel responds by giving God thanks and praise for granting his specific request: "To You, O God of my fathers, I give thanks and praise, for You have given me wisdom and power; even now You have made known to me what we requested of You, for You have made known to us the king's matter" (Dan. 2:23).

> When we are in anxiety-inducing circumstances, we should figure out what we need and take those needs to God in prayer.

In the book of 1 Chronicles, we are reminded of this aspect of prayer in the middle of a genealogy list. We are told that Jabez specifically asked God to do several things in his life: "Now Jabez called on the God of Israel, saying, 'Oh that You would bless me indeed and enlarge my border, and that Your hand might be with me, and that You would keep me from harm that it might not pain me!'" (4:10). The chronicler then adds, "And God granted him what he requested" (4:10c).

In David's messianic psalm, the Lord says to us as co-heirs with Christ: "Ask of Me, and I will surely give the nations as Your inheritance, and the very ends of the earth as Your possession" (Ps. 2:8). When we lack wisdom in life's trials, we are told to ask Him for wisdom. He also commands us to ask in faith with the promise that wisdom will be granted to us (James 1:5–8). Similarly, the Lord Jesus encourages us to ask God for what we need. He says:

> *Ask*, and it will be given to you; seek, and you will find; knock, and it will be opened to you. For everyone who *asks* receives, and he who seeks finds, and to him who knocks it will be opened. Or what man is there among you who, when his son *asks*

for a loaf, will give him a stone? Or if he *asks* for a fish, he will not give him a snake, will he? If you then, being evil, know how to give good gifts to your children, how much more will your Father who is in heaven give what is good to those who *ask* Him! (Matt. 7:7–11, emphasis added)

In the above passage, *asking* is compared to *seeking* and *knocking*. At first glance, it seems that the imperatives to "ask," "seek," and "knock" are actions that we do once before leaving the matter with the Lord. But all these verbs are present imperatives and therefore convey the idea of continuous action: keep on asking, keep on seeking, and keep on knocking. The continuous action of the verbs grows in intensity and focus.

In a sermon on Luke 11:9–10, the British preacher Charles Spurgeon talked about asking, seeking, and knocking as three levels of depth in prayer:

Now observe that these varieties of prayer are put on an ascending scale. It is said first that we ask—I suppose that refers to the prayer which is a mere statement of our needs in which we tell the Lord that we need this and that and ask Him to grant it to us. But as we learn the art of prayer we go on further to seek—which signifies that we marshal our arguments and plead reasons for the granting of our desires—and we begin to wrestle with God for the mercies needed. And if the blessings come not, we then rise to the third degree which is knocking—we become importunate—we are not content with asking and giving reasons, but we throw the whole earnestness of our being into our requests and practice the text which says, "the kingdom of Heaven suffers violence and the violent take it by force."[3]

The Lord Jesus stresses the need for our persistence, perseverance, and earnestness in asking. In addition, we are told in Matthew 7:7 that those who habitually ask will receive; those who habitually seek will find; and to those who habitually knock, it shall be opened. Our heavenly Father is the request-granting God. God answers prayer.

It's important to add that there is a danger of misusing this promise as carte blanche for selfish requests (James 4:3). Jesus is talking about making our requests with

God-honoring motives.

Perhaps one of the reasons we do not make specific requests in the midst of our anxiety is that we are not expecting our heavenly Father to actually answer prayer. In

> True prayer is expecting God to do something, looking for His answers.

With Christ in the School of Prayer, Andrew Murray points out one of the symptoms of a deep illness of practical atheism in the church. He writes:

> One of the terrible marks of the diseased state of Christian life these days is that there are so many who are content *without distinct the experience of answer to prayer*. They pray daily, they *ask* many things, and they trust that some of them will be heard. But they know little of direct definite answer to prayer as the rule of daily life. . . . Prayer is supposed to have an answer.[4] (emphasis added)

Therefore, expecting answers from God in the midst of anxiety, we let our requests be made known to Him when we need wisdom for facing a particular issue. In the various scenarios of our lives, we are to intentionally think through what we want God to provide, and then ask Him—humbly, fervently, expectantly, and persistently.

These are requests. They are specific and arise out of real needs and concerns. God's children expect their Father to answer. True prayer is not just getting on our knees, uttering pious platitudes, or engaging in therapeutic mystical babbling. Rather, it is expecting God to do something, looking for His answers. By the means of prayer and supplication with thanksgiving, we make our requests known to God.

TRUSTING AND TALKING
TO GOD THROUGH TURBULENCE

The words "to God" are more significant than they seem. The directive to make our requests known to God does not mean that God was previously uninformed. He knows all things past, present, future, potential—completely and exhaustively. Tozer writes:

God knows instantly and effortlessly all matter and all matters, all mind and every mind, all spirit and all spirits, all being and every being, all creaturehood and all creatures, every plurality and all plurality, all law and every law, all relations, all causes, all thoughts, all mysteries, all enigmas, all feeling, all desires, every unuttered secret, all thrones and dominions, all personalities, all things visible, and invisible in heaven and in earth, motion, space, time, life, death, good, evil, heaven, and hell.[5]

But our God is not an omniscient computer or an infinite Mr. Spock. His omniscience is a caring omniscience. Tozer captures this well:

Our Father in heaven knows our frame and remembers that we are dust. He knew our inborn treachery, and for His own sake engaged to save us (Isa. 48:8–11). His only begotten Son, when He walked among us, felt our pains in their naked intensity of anguish. His knowledge of our afflictions and adversities is more than theoretic; it is personal, warm, and compassionate. Whatever may befall us, God knows and cares as no one else can.[6]

Our all-knowing heavenly Father wants us to trust Him and depend on Him. The fact that our Father already knows our needs and cares is a major incentive for believing prayer and trust in Him (Matt. 6:32–33). He wants us to talk to Him, sharing our hearts and needs and troubles with Him.

Prayer is one of the most vital expressions of our trust in and dependence on God.

When you take that final step onto an airplane, you are placing your life in the hands of the pilot, crew, and flight attendants. There is much that we may not understand about aviation, air currents, plane engines, and everything else involved in flying, but we buckle our seat belt and settle in for the flight as a matter of faith. Sometimes we fly through turbulence, and we feel the plane and ourselves shaking at the high altitude! If we need help or reassurances, we call on the flight attendant, and they help us. We trust that they can.

Similarly, prayer is one of the most vital expressions of our trust in and dependence on God. God our Father is the pilot! We are not just souls on the plane of faith; we are His children. By His grace and power, we will reach our destination: glory. He is also sovereign and all-powerful. He is in control of the turbulence, and every bit of turbulence that we feel on the flight of faith is either permitted or sent directly by Him for His glory and our good! We can, therefore, call on Him in faith. In faith, we tell Him about all of our worrisome problems and turbulent circumstances. We humble ourselves and give all our cares and worries to the Lord (1 Peter 5:7). Do you remember the words of the famous hymn?

What a Friend we have in Jesus,
All our sins and griefs to bear!
What a privilege to carry
Everything to God in prayer![7]

This hymn reminds us of the privilege and benefit of carrying everything to the Lord in prayer. We see the same call to prayer in our key passage. Notice how the passage reads: "Be anxious for nothing, but in everything by prayer and supplication with thanksgiving let your requests be made known to God." Let's not give God the silent treatment.

4

A Precious Promise for Hard-Pressed People

And the peace of God, which surpasses all comprehension,
will guard your hearts and your minds in Christ Jesus.

PHILIPPIANS 4:7

So far we have considered two biblical components of God's practical strategy to overcome worry—turning off the faucet of anxiety and turning to prayer. But one more element remains: *God's peace*. Worry is overcome by expecting peace from God. Anxiety is conquered by anticipating the protecting power of God's peace.

Philippians 4:7 reads: "And the peace of God, which surpasses all comprehension, will guard your hearts and your minds in Christ Jesus." These words have been a source of strength for God's people for the last two thousand years. They are some of the first words of Scripture many anxious Christians memorize. They have served as the North Star for many Christians experiencing a dark night of the soul.

The truths in this verse have stood the test of time. But our familiarity with these encouraging words has the potential to lessen their radical and unexpected edge as a strategy for overcoming worry. The words of Scripture have penetrated the collective mind of the Western world for the last two thousand years and, as a result, their original and startlingly subversive power may be lost on us. We must interact with this passage and the rest of Scripture as if we are interacting with them for the first time in order to realize how wonderfully subversive the Scriptures are.

In our human understanding, we might have preferred Paul to end this passage with something like, "and God will grant your requests and solve your problem." But in this text, God does not utter one word about changing our circumstances. Instead, He promises to grant us peace right in the middle of anxiety-inducing circumstances.

Think about this promise. It is both precious and subversive. It is a precious promise for hard-pressed people. Yet it also subverts our obsession with seeing our problems resolved and our difficulties disappear. Our focus is redirected to God Himself and His promise of peace. Of course, our heavenly Father is not indifferent to our difficulty, nor does He lack pity for our pain. Peace does not preclude praying for changed circumstances. But the point is the Lord uses anxiety-inducing circumstances as teachable moments in order to teach us to trust Him.

There is no situation so dark that God, who is greater than our circumstances, cannot be trusted. Peace in the midst of difficulty, along with the development of character—this is what matters to the Lord.

> The Lord Jesus may indeed change our circumstances, but He does that according to His purpose and timing, not ours.

Experience of His peace is evidence of faith, growth, and maturity. After believing prayer comes the surprising experience of peace. The Lord Jesus may indeed change our circumstances, but He does that according to His purpose and timing, not ours.

Consider the word *and*, which Paul uses to begin this verse. Paul rarely uses the conjunction *and* to connect sentences in his writings. So the fact that he does so here is noteworthy: "Be anxious for nothing, but in everything by prayer and supplication with thanksgiving let your requests be made known to God. *And* the peace of God, which surpasses all comprehension, will guard your hearts and your minds in Christ Jesus" (emphasis added). Paul's use of this word makes it clear to us that peace in the midst of life's difficulties is the direct result of grateful, faith-based praying.

As God's children pray to their heavenly Father and have the Spirit-empowered audacity to take God at His word, God will respond and grant peace. As the Lord filled the tabernacle of old with the cloud of His glory, so the Lord will fill the tabernacle of your heart with the cloud of His peace in response to prayer throughout your journey in the desert of anxiety.

PUZZLED BUT PEACEFUL

Our capacity for experiencing peace is not contingent on our limited human understanding. It does not depend on our ability to fill in all of the blanks or connect the dots in our personal experiences. Peace is not contingent on our skill in understanding the hand of God's providence in our life. Whether we like it or not, we are limited in many ways as human beings by the constraints of finitude. No matter how experienced or how well-educated or how well-travelled, we do not know everything. Only God is omniscient. But even when we cannot understand the hand of God's providence, we can trust His heart and experience His peace.

The Puzzle of Life

Because of this narrow and finite vantage point, life sometimes seems strange and puzzling. We desperately cry out to God about our problems, pain, and perplexing circumstances, often asking for (or demanding) an explanation. Although it is clear from Scripture that suffering produces Christlike character in us (see Heb. 5:8; Rom. 5:3–5; James 1:2–4; Rom. 8:28–30) and that we will never be forsaken in our trials (Heb. 13:5), the Lord does not promise to explain why we are going through the waters of difficulty in this life. Instead, our heavenly Father reminds us of His character. He is good, wise, holy, righteous, omnipotent, omnipresent, and omniscient. What matters is who He is.

> Experiencing the peace of God is not a result of finding all of the pieces to the puzzle of life. Peace is the result of trust.

As we learn to trust the Lord, to stake our very soul for all time and eternity on the plain teaching of His Word, we see that our quest for clarity is futile and that we cannot put the enigmatic jigsaw puzzles of our lives together. But experiencing the peace of God is not a result of finding all of the pieces to the puzzle of life. Peace is the result of trust. I find this spiritual reality to be an immense encouragement.

Peace with God

As we discuss peace, it is important for us to understand the difference between peace *with* God (Rom. 5:1) and the peace *of* God (Phil. 4:7). All believers have peace with God, and we should praise God for this fundamental reality. Peace with God is the result of being made right with God by faith. When we trust Christ as our personal Lord and Savior, at that moment, in and through Christ, we become all that God requires us to be, which we could never be through our own effort. The result of this stupendous transaction is peace *with* God. The vain and selfish war we waged against God is over, and we are no longer His enemies.

The Peace of God

However, not all followers of Christ enduringly know and experience the peace *of* God. While peace with God is the result of salvation, our ability to experience the peace of God is a result of our ongoing choice to exercise faith and trust, living life in the power of the Spirit.

Philippians 4:7 is the only place in Scripture where the expression "the peace of God" is used. Paul uses a similar statement in Col. 3:15: "Let the peace of Christ rule [or act as arbitrator] in your hearts." When interpersonal tensions threaten to disrupt the unity of our local church life, we are to submit ourselves to the peace of

Christ and allow His peace to regulate the mutual inter-personal relations of our church life. The Lord Jesus calls us to peace, not strife, in our relationships with one another (Col. 3:15).

In Philippians 4:7, "the peace of God" is a descriptive statement about God Himself. It is hard to even begin to understand the significance of these words. The peace of God is the awesome well-being, the glorious serenity, the inexpressible wholeness, and the inner tranquility that characterize the infinite being of God Himself. Since God is omnipotent, His peace is an all-powerful peace. Since God is eternal, His peace is without beginning or end. Since God is infinite, His peace is limitless. Since God is holy, His peace is pure. From everlasting to everlasting this peace has marked and permeated the august being of God.

And the peace *of* God is not only a breathtaking description of our Lord's inner life; it also means that God is the giver, producer, and source of peace. He is the only one in the universe who produces peace. The peace that describes Him, He also produces and gives to us by His Spirit (Gal. 5:22) in response to our trusting prayers. Our experience of the peace of God is the in-breaking of God

Himself in the life of the Christian.

Paul goes on to describe peace as "the peace of God, which surpasses all comprehension." In light of the nature of God's peace, such an observation is not surprising! All of the finite understanding

> The peace of God is the awesome well-being, the glorious serenity, the inexpressible wholeness, and the inner tranquility that characterize the infinite being of God Himself.

of the universe, both angelic and human, does not have the capacity to measure the depths, scale the heights, or traverse the breadth of God's peace. And as we've discussed, God the Father grants us His peace right in the throes of difficulty. But what does this look like practically in real life?

Many years ago, I worked as an X-ray technician in a local hospital in Chicago. One morning, a young woman was wheeled into my X-ray room in a hospital bed. It was not uncommon for me to see patients both young and old brought to me in hospital beds, so I was not expecting anything out of the ordinary with this patient. I helped her move from her hospital bed onto the examination table. She glanced at me, but I had the impression that she didn't really see me. She was like someone standing on the beach looking out at dark and menacing clouds on the horizon.

Before I could begin the process of taking X-rays, she suddenly blurted out, "I just learned I have a terminal illness. They just told me that I am going to die; I am terrified."

I felt great sadness for her. I did not have much time, but prompted by the Lord, I took a breath, looked at her and said, "God loves you. He gave His Son, Jesus, to die on the cross for you. Jesus is alive, risen from among the dead. If you trust Him as your personal Lord and Savior, you will go to heaven when you die."

The young lady trusted Christ as Lord and Savior on that X-ray table, and it was immediately obvious that something had changed. She looked at me and declared, "I have peace now! I have peace now." Her circumstances had not changed. She was still terminally sick, but God stepped in and gave her peace that surpassed all understanding. There was no noise, no fanfare, but like the silent power of a sunrise, the Sun of Righteousness cast His healing rays over the inner world of this young woman.

After the procedure was over, they wheeled her out of the room, and I never saw her again. But there was a supernatural procedure that took place in the room that morning, and this young lady went on her way rejoicing. I look forward to seeing her in heaven!

If you are not in a relationship with God though faith in Christ, there is good news for you. What the Lord Jesus did for that young lady, He can and will do for you if you trust Him as your personal Lord and Savior. He promises to give us peace that surpasses all understanding right in the center of our difficulties. I have seen Him do it over and over again.

Remember, the blessing of peace is available only to those who are in Christ Jesus, to those who are in union with Him. It is those who know and trust Christ, willingly submitted to Him, who experience God's peace in the midst of worry. Being in Christ is central to everything.

When I was in the army many years ago, I worked in the hospital on the base of Fort Sam Houston in Texas. One morning at about two o'clock, as I was working the third shift, I was called up to the ward to take an X-ray of a man. When I arrived in his room, I was stunned by what I saw. He was lying in bed struggling to breathe, and his body was burning with fever. I knew this soldier likely did not have much time left. He was hanging over the precipice of eternity.

> When lost people see the Christian community enjoying peace in the midst of difficulty, they may ask questions.

I felt compelled to tell him that God loves him and that He has given His Son, Jesus, to die on the cross for all of his sins. I shared the good news that if he would repent and trust Christ as His personal Lord and Savior, God would save him immediately, giving him the gift of eternal life.

Then I witnessed this man struggling to breathe, burning up with fever, yet raising his hands up in praise to God as a visible sign of his trust in Christ. I saw this man at the edge of the abyss experience the supernatural peace of God!

I went downstairs to develop the X-ray, and when I returned with the X-ray about fifteen minutes later, the man was dead. Just like the criminal on the cross, God can grant peace to people who trust Christ even at the very end of life. What a mighty God we serve. He is truly the God of peace!

You see, the depth of God's peace that floods the spirits of trusting Christians is not of this world. It comes from God Himself through the power and ministry of the Holy Spirit. And God's peace supersedes our circumstances.

PEACE AS AN APOLOGETIC

People in the so-called postmodern and post-Christian world may not be interested in God, but they are interested in spirituality. It is not uncommon for twenty-first-century people to claim that they are spiritual. We should welcome this as a wonderful bridge to the gospel. Our individual and corporate experience of peace becomes a witness for the reality of Christ.

As we demonstrate that it is possible to live a life that is victorious over worry because of our experience of the peace of God through the power and ministry of the Holy Spirit, our lives become a powerful evangelistic and apologetic tool. When lost people see the Christian community enjoying peace in the midst of difficulty, they may ask questions. The very peace of the redeemed community is an apologetic, that is, a reason we may offer to people for our trust in Christ. Our experience of peace becomes a testimony, pointing unbelievers to Jesus (Acts 4:8–12). As we read in 1 Peter 3:15, "Sanctify Christ as Lord in your hearts, always being ready to make a defense to everyone who asks you to give an account for the hope that is in you, yet with gentleness and reverence."

THE PROTECTING POWER OF PEACE

Finally, the peace of God that surpasses all understanding is a *protecting* peace. Paul explains that the peace of God will guard our hearts and minds in Christ Jesus. The verb translated *guard* is a military term, which was used for a detachment of soldiers that protected a city from attack. Since Philippi was a Roman colony, a group of Roman soldiers would have been stationed there in order to protect the city from attack by their enemies. The Philippians would have understood the import of this guard duty imagery immediately. The verb *guard* illustrates and personifies God's peace as a heavenly detachment of soldiers, sent from heaven with the mission to protect the vulnerable city of our hearts and minds from the vicious assaults and attacks of worry. When worrisome situations and circumstances attack, our hearts and minds are easy targets. But God's peace will protect our emotional and mental world from the drones and snipers of worry.

During recent presidential inaugural celebrations, newly elected presidents of the United States ride in protected limousines as they move up Pennsylvania Avenue on the way to the White House. The presidential motorcade is always impressive. Cars, along with motorcycles, are in front and in back of the presidential limousine. Secret Service personnel run alongside the president's limo in order to provide protection en route to the White House.

As Christians, we may not be the president of the

United States, but we are royalty. You are in Christ, elected in Him before the foundation of the world. You have taken your seat in the limousine of salvation. As you struggle to move up the Pennsylvania Avenue of life en route to your heavenly Father's house, the peace of God will guard your heart and mind from the vicious assaults of worry.

5

Walking in Freedom from Worry

Do not be anxious about anything, but in every situation, by prayer and petition, with thanksgiving, present your requests to God. And the peace of God, which transcends all understanding, will guard your hearts and your minds in Christ Jesus.

PHILIPPIANS 4:6–7 NIV

A number of years ago, my family and I went to Six Flags Great America, where I decided to face one of my childhood anxieties by taking a ride on one of the towering roller coasters. I stood in line and then took my seat in the roller coaster car, my wife sitting next to me.

As we sat in our car, a sturdy metallic arm came down in front of us and locked us in. A few moments later, our roller coaster car started moving forward. I can still hear the dreadful clicking sounds as we crept higher, higher, and higher up a steep incline. As we neared the top, I looked out over the horizon and noticed the houses were getting smaller. The higher we got, the more my anxiety rose.

We finally reached the top of the roller coaster, and I looked down—big mistake! Before I had an opportunity to process what I'd seen, we made a sharp turn, and the next thing I knew, we were flying down a steep track at breakneck speed!

I slammed my eyes shut, screamed at the top of my lungs, and held on to that roller coaster arm with all of my might. Somehow I mustered the courage to open my eyes as we headed into loop after loop. I didn't know whether I was up or down. I was dizzy, and fatigue forced me to release my grip on the metallic arm. I slouched in my car, thinking, *I can't take any more. I can't take any more. I am going to black out . . .*

Just as I was getting ready to pass out, the ride came to a stop! The roller coaster designer must have known just how much we could take. I was so relieved that it was over!

THE ROLLER COASTER OF LIFE

Sometimes life feels like a roller coaster. There may be times when we're on the straightaway, and it's easy to remain calm and trust God. Then life takes a sharp turn, and we find ourselves flying through difficulty at breakneck speed, doing everything we can do to hold on while the tides of worry rise in our hearts. We finally get the courage to open our eyes and look life in the face, only to see ourselves going through a loop of financial setback, a loop of loss, a loop of illness. We don't know if we are up or if we are down, and it seems like our lives are getting upended. We think, *I can't take any more. I can't take any more, Jesus!*

But you know what? When we stop worrying and commit ourselves to God in prayer, something incredible happens. The Lord will give us peace. And in God's own time, the ride

> Each season of life brings its own unique roller coaster of anxiety. This will be our reality until we walk through the doors of glory.

will come to a stop! Our heavenly Father knows just how much we can take. We will find ourselves experiencing calm moments, but each season of life brings its own unique roller coaster of anxiety. This will be our reality until we walk through the doors of glory.

Yet no matter how steep the incline or how fast the descent, you can't be thrown off the roller coaster because the arms of God have locked you in. In fact, nothing can separate us from the love of God in Christ Jesus our Lord (Rom. 8:31–39).

LET'S GET PRACTICAL

So far we've learned about God's strategy for overcoming worry: Stop worrying. Pray about everything. Anticipate the peace of God. But practically, *how do we begin to put these steps into practice?*

Biblical Meditation

The spiritual discipline of meditation should not be confused with Eastern meditation. In Eastern or transcendental meditation, a person attempts to empty the mind of thought and emotion in order to become one with the so-called cosmic consciousness. In the practice of Eastern meditation, active mental effort is intentionally switched off, and a person is consequently exposed to whatever external impressions may come. The practice is fraught with danger. In this passive frame of mind, a person may open themselves to demonic powers and influences.

On the other hand, biblical meditation involves rigorous and prolonged reflection on the *person* of God, the *character* of God, and the *ways* of God. In biblical meditation, one chooses a portion of Scripture and thinks hard about the passage, reflecting slowly and deeply about the content of the passage and its practical implications for living. In biblical meditation, you are in an active frame of mind, filling your mind with the Scriptures. The Lord Himself commanded Joshua to habitually meditate on His Word: "This book of the law shall not depart from your mouth, but you shall *meditate*

> Habitual meditation on the Word of God is one of the hallmarks of the blessed person in Psalm 1:2.

on it day and night" (Josh. 1:8, emphasis added).

Habitual meditation on the Word of God is one of the hallmarks of the blessed person in Psalm 1:2. In Psalm 63:1–8, we see David's desire for God Himself, which is fueled as he remembers God on his bed and meditates upon God in the night watches. Instead of allowing his mind to wander into the dark woods of faulty thinking, David fills his mind with thoughts of God. He gives lengthy and prolonged mental consideration to God's person, character, and ways. The Psalms have much more to say about the practice of biblical meditation (see Pss. 1:2; 4:4; 63:6; 104:34; 119:15, 23, 48, 78, 97, 99, 148; 143:5–6). So we see that deep and prolonged thinking about the Lord's Word, person, and work is biblical and is an integral part of our walk as Christians. Christ followers have practiced biblical meditation for centuries, but our generation has by and large forgotten the vital role that meditation plays in Christian thinking and living. Meditation is critical because whatever shapes our thinking also shapes our lives and characters.

Reflection on the Scriptures allows God's Word to penetrate our minds and our emotions, to soften our hard hearts and wills. J. I. Packer notes the purpose of meditation:

> Its purpose is to clear one's mental and spiritual vision of God, and to let his truth make its full and proper impact on one's mind and heart. It is a matter of talking to oneself about God and one-self; it is, indeed, often a matter of arguing with oneself, reasoning oneself out of moods of doubt and unbelief into a clear apprehension of God's power and grace.[1]

Through biblical meditation, you can cultivate the habit of thinking about Him who matters most in life. When you face anxiety-inducing circumstances, take the words "be anxious for nothing," and ponder them throughout the day.

What if, when we awoke in the middle of the night and couldn't sleep, we meditated on these truths? What if, instead of automatically turning on the TV, playing with our smartphones, or killing time on Facebook or Twitter, we meditated on these powerful words instead?

May the Holy Spirit open our eyes to understand the

good news woven into the imperative. (See Appendix B for more Scriptures on which to meditate and ponder when you are battling worry.)

Prayer in Practice

Some of us need to take an inventory of our lives. Is there a problem, a struggle, or an interpersonal relationship that is causing anxiety in your life for which you have not yet prayed? Is there some area in your life that is troubling you, but you have not talked to God about it?

> Getting to know God better through prayer is essential to conquering anxiety.

One way to be proactive in prayer is to write out your requests. Requests presuppose that we have given some thought to these matters before the Lord. Keep a list of granted requests and answered prayer.

When I was in a prayer meeting where we regularly shared our prayer requests aloud, every week a woman named Klara kept a list of the requests, and the following week, she would ask the group, "What happened? Did God grant the request?" She was expecting something from God.

The hymn "What a Friend We Have in Jesus" powerfully communicates the biblical truths we have been exploring. Read the words of this hymn and heartily sing to the Lord. And through singing, take your worries and anxieties to God in prayer. Anxiety is conquered by picking up the phone of faith and having a talk with God. And Jesus will always answer the phone. A. W. Tozer wrote:

> In coming to Him at any time we need not wonder whether we shall find Him in a receptive mood. He is always receptive to misery and need, as well as to love and faith. He does not keep office hours nor set aside periods when He will see no one.[2]

Keep the Channel of Communication with Heaven Open

Living in sin and disobedience hinders our prayer life (James 4:3; 1 Peter 3:7). Sin does not change the standing of a Christian with God (Eph. 1:7; Heb. 10:15–18), but it interrupts our fellowship with our heavenly Father (1 John 1:6–7).

Since prayer is such a vital part of Christian living, we must examine ourselves and repent of sin and confess it to our heavenly Father. Repentance and confession are how we keep the channel of communication with Him open and unhindered (1 John 1:9; Rev. 2:4–5, 14–16, 22; 3:3, 19).

Increase Your Prayer Time

How much time do we spend in prayer each day? For many of us, the time set aside for prayer adds up to only a few minutes daily, which I think leaves much to be desired. We cannot generalize, but many Christians in America do not have a robust prayer life. While we should not be legalistic in our prayer lives, there is a clear call in Scripture to regular and dedicated prayer (Col. 4:2–3).

Another way to expand your prayer time is to pray through the Psalms. I would recommend beginning with Psalm 31, which highlights trusting the Lord in the midst of distress and alarm. You can also read and pray through A. W. Tozer's book *The Knowledge of the Holy*. Each chapter is a wonderful study of a different attribute of God. I have prayed through this book for the last thirty years, and the Lord has met me in wonderful ways as I have done so.

As thanksgiving and praise become a daily part of your prayer life, you will grow in the knowledge of God. Getting to know God better through prayer is essential to conquering anxiety.

Prayers of Surrender

Prayer does not always mean that the Lord will remove the difficulty you are facing. Sometimes He does not. This reality is laid out for us in 2 Corinthians 12:7–10, where Paul shares that he was given a thorn in the flesh. We are not told the specifics of the thorn, but we see that Paul sought the Lord three times about this particular matter in prayer. He requested that the thorn be taken away, but God's answer was no. But with God's no came a better plan.

Think deeply about the promise of God that holds true in all circumstances of life: "My grace is sufficient for you" (2 Cor. 12:9).

AN ANCIENT BENEDICTION

To aid you in your battle against worry, I have provided a list of Scriptures in Appendix B so that you will "be transformed by the renewing of your mind" (Rom. 12:2) as you battle worry. In Appendix A, you will find a simple pattern for prayer to be used as you seek the peace of God in the midst of various situations and trials. And finally, for questions to enhance your own reflection on the teaching in this book or to aid in discussion with your small group, go to Appendix C.

And now I would like to do what I do at the end of every church service at Judson Baptist Church, where I currently serve as pastor. I give a benediction. I cannot convey blessing—only Jesus can do that—but on His behalf, I have the privilege to speak words of blessing to His people. And to every anxious Christian, I want to speak the words of the ancient but timeless benediction:

> The LORD bless you, and keep you;
>
> The LORD make His face shine on you,
> And be gracious to you;
>
> The LORD lift up His countenance on you,
> And give you peace. (Num. 6:24–26)

Appendix A

A Pattern for Prayer

The different seasons and responsibilities of life bring with them their own anxieties. This section will close with a pattern of prayer that you may follow no matter what season you are in and regardless of your circumstances.

Maybe you are a father. You have major responsibilities as the servant leader of your home, and perhaps life is not what you expected it to be. You toss and turn during the night, unable to sleep, trying to figure out how you are going to make ends meet. You may be so worried that you haven't had a good night's rest in months. Worry has settled into your heart, and tension has spilled over into your relationships with your wife and children. You may be frustrated because you feel that the deck of life was stacked against you from the very beginning. You think you are losing at the game of life. Dad, it's time to get on your knees. Tell God about everything that is troubling you. Talk to God about it, trust Him, take Him at His word, and God will give you peace. The situation may or may not change, but your wife and your family will know that you have changed. You will be able to lead your family and guide them in experiencing the peace of God.

Maybe you are a mother who feels overwhelmed by fear for your children. Not an hour goes by that you're not worrying about your child's safety in this dangerous world. You worry about your children especially when you are apart and you aren't present to care for them. Or maybe you are consumed with worry over the futures of your children. What if they don't get good grades, can't get into college, or what if there aren't any jobs when they graduate? Mom, whatever your fear, talk to the Lord about your concerns and choose to walk in faith. Entrust your son or your daughter to God, and the Lord will give you peace. Be concerned, but stop worrying.

Maybe you are a good and loving parent, and you've raised your children in the fear and admonition of the Lord—and yet your teenage son or daughter has walked away from Him. You were not a perfect parent, but you were good to your children. Suddenly it seems your child is rejecting Christ. They disrespect you or say terrible things to you. Or you all are constantly fighting with one another. You frequently find them missing from their room late into the night and early morning. Your phone calls go unanswered, and you toss and turn for the remainder of the night. Parent, get on your knees in faith, and talk to the Lord about your wayward child. Entrust your son or your daughter to God, and the Lord will give you peace. Be concerned, but stop worrying.

Maybe you finally got your dream job. You worked your way through college, studying hard. Perhaps you did an internship in your area of study and the company hired you upon graduation, or you've worked your way up over the course of years. But out of nowhere, performance anxiety is rising up in your heart. You are so worried, and you don't have peace. Stop worrying, talk to God about it in faith, and expect His peace.

Maybe you are going to have major surgery or a medical procedure next week. You may be afraid, but you have entrusted yourself to God and you have peace. But your unsaved relatives and friends don't understand. And you find it incredible that God has given you the kind of peace that you have. You are learning firsthand that no circumstance is greater than God's peace. And you have the opportunity to be a witness to those friends and family members. Let your faith and trust shine a light among them to point the way to Jesus Christ.

As you take these and other concerns before the Lord in prayer, whatever your circumstances, pray in faith, and expect that God will give you peace.

Father in heaven, we come before You now in the almighty name of Jesus. We come with our concerns. You have graciously commanded us in Your Word to "be anxious for nothing." But we have real concerns and problems in our lives that trouble us. We confess that we are struggling with worry in this situation. Thank You that we can bring all of our concerns to You. We bring to You the concern of _____. We shed tears of distress as we talk to You about this. Please provide for all of our needs in this situation, Father. In the meantime, would You please help us to seek first Your kingdom and Your righteousness, knowing that in Your own time, You will care for all of our needs? We are thankful that You have provided for us to this point. You have provided for us in ways that we did not expect. We thank You for Your ongoing care, concern, and provision. And we expect You to give us Your peace as we walk through these difficulties with You.

O righteous Father, in our pit of worry, we confess that we have found fault and been discontented with You. But we bless Your name for Your self-revelation in Philippians 4:6–7. You are in control. You are able to grant us peace in any situation in life. We therefore retract the foolishness we uttered, and we repent of our worry and sinful self-reliance. Help us to care deeply without slipping into worry. We have prayed to You in faith, and we thank You in advance for the protecting power of Your peace in our hearts and minds today. And with the psalmist we pray: "But as for me, I trust in You, O LORD, I say, 'You are my God.' My times are in your hand" (Ps. 31:14–15a).

Appendix B

Scriptures to Aid in Your Battle against Worry

Be anxious for nothing, but in everything by prayer and supplication with thanksgiving let your requests be made known to God. And the peace of God, which surpasses all comprehension, will guard your hearts and your minds in Christ Jesus.

Philippians 4:6–7

To You, O Lord, I lift up my soul.
O my God, in You I trust,
Do not let me be ashamed;
Do not let my enemies exult over me.
Indeed, none of those who wait for You will be
    ashamed;
Those who deal treacherously without cause will be
    ashamed.

Make me know Your ways, O LORD;
Teach me Your paths.
Lead me in Your truth and teach me,
For You are the God of my salvation;
For You I wait all the day.

Psalm 25:1–5

Then they cried to the LORD in their trouble,
And He brought them out of their distresses.
He caused the storm to be still,
So that the waves of the sea were hushed.

Psalm 107:28–29

Therefore I urge you, brethren, by the mercies of God, to present your bodies a living and holy sacrifice, acceptable to God, which is your spiritual service of worship. And do not be conformed to this world, but be transformed by the renewing of your mind, so that you may prove what the will of God is, that which is good and acceptable and perfect.

Romans 12:1–2

Now may the God of hope fill you with all joy and peace in believing, so that you will abound in hope by the power of the Holy Spirit.

Romans 15:13

For this reason I say to you, do not be worried about your life, as to what you will eat or what you will drink; nor for your body, as to what you will put on. Is not life more than food, and the body more than clothing? Look at the birds of the air, that they do not sow, nor reap nor gather into barns, and yet your heavenly Father feeds them. Are you not worth much more than they? And who of you by being worried can add a single hour to his life? . . . Do not worry then, saying, "What will we eat?" or "What will we drink?" or "What will we wear for clothing?" For . . . your heavenly Father knows that you need all these things. But seek first His kingdom and His righteousness, and all these things will be added to you. So do not worry about tomorrow; for tomorrow will care for itself. Each day has enough trouble of its own.

Matthew 6:25–27, 31–34

Therefore humble yourselves under the mighty hand of God, that He may exalt you at the proper time, casting all your anxiety on Him, because He cares for you.

1 Peter 5:6–7

The LORD is my shepherd; I shall not want. He makes me lie down in green pastures. He leads me beside still waters. He restores my soul. He leads me in paths of righteousness for his name's sake. Even though I walk through the valley of the shadow of death, I will fear no evil, for you are with me; your rod and your staff, they comfort me. You prepare a table before me in the presence of my enemies; you anoint my head with oil; my cup overflows. Surely goodness and mercy shall follow me all the days of my life, and I shall dwell in the house of the LORD forever.

Psalm 23 ESV

Those who love Your law have great peace,
And nothing causes them to stumble.

Psalm 119:165

Whatever you do in word or deed, do all in the name of the Lord Jesus, giving thanks through Him to God the Father.

Colossians 3:17

Make sure that your character is free from the love of money, being content with what you have; for He Himself has said, "I will never desert you, nor will I ever forsake you," so that we confidently say, "The Lord is my helper, I will not be afraid. What will man do to me?"

Hebrews 13:5–6

But the fruit of the Spirit is love, joy, peace, patience, kindness, goodness, faithfulness, gentleness, self-control; against such things there is no law.

Galatians 5:22–23

Therefore, having been justified by faith, we have peace with God through our Lord Jesus Christ, through whom also we have obtained our introduction by faith into this grace in which we stand; and we exult in hope of the glory of God. And not only this, but we also exult in our tribulations, knowing that tribulation brings about perseverance; and perseverance, proven character; and proven character, hope; and hope does not disappoint, because the love of God has been poured out within our hearts through the Holy Spirit who was given to us.

Romans 5:1–5

Now may the God of hope fill you with all joy and peace in believing, so that you will abound in hope by the power of the Holy Spirit.

Romans 15:13

Let the peace of Christ rule in your hearts, to which indeed you were called in one body; and be thankful.

Colossians 3:15

Finally, brethren, rejoice, be made complete, be comforted, be like-minded, live in peace; and the God of love and peace will be with you.

2 Corinthians 13:11

For the sake of the truth which abides in us and will be with us forever: Grace, mercy and peace will be with us, from God the Father and from Jesus Christ, the Son of the Father, in truth and love.

2 John 2–3

Finally, brothers and sisters, whatever is true, whatever is noble, whatever is right, whatever is pure, whatever is lovely, whatever is admirable—if anything is excellent or praiseworthy—think about such things.

Philippians 4:8 NIV

You will keep him in perfect peace,
Whose mind is stayed on You,
Because he trusts in You.
Trust in the LORD forever,
For in YAH, the LORD, is everlasting strength.

Isaiah 26:3–4 NKJV

Do not let your heart be troubled; believe in God, believe also in Me.

John 14:1

Strengthen the weak hands,
and make firm the feeble knees.
Say to those who are of a fearful heart,
"Be strong, fear not!
Behold, your God
will come with vengeance,
with the recompense of God.
He will come and save you."

Isaiah 35:3–4 RSV

Peace I leave with you; my peace I give to you; not as the world gives do I give to you. Let not your hearts be troubled, neither let them be afraid.

John 14:27 RSV

My flesh and my heart may fail,
but God is the strength of my heart and my portion for ever.

Psalm 73:26 RSV

In peace I will both lie down and sleep,
For You alone, O LORD, make me to dwell in safety.

Psalm 4:8

SCRIPTURES TO AID IN YOUR BATTLE AGAINST WORRY

What, then, shall we say in response to these things? If God is for us, who can be against us? He who did not spare his own Son, but gave him up for us all— how will he not also, along with him, graciously give us all things? Who will bring any charge against those whom God has chosen? It is God who justifies. Who then is the one who condemns? No one. Christ Jesus who died—more than that, who was raised to life— is at the right hand of God and is also interceding for us. Who shall separate us from the love of Christ? Shall trouble or hardship or persecution or famine or nakedness or danger or sword? As it is written: "For your sake we face death all day long; we are considered as sheep to be slaughtered." No, in all these things we are more than conquerors through him who loved us. For I am convinced that neither death nor life, neither angels nor demons, neither the present nor the future, nor any powers, neither height nor depth, nor anything else in all creation, will be able to separate us from the love of God that is in Christ Jesus our Lord.

Romans 8:31–39 NIV

Now may the God of peace who brought again from the dead our Lord Jesus, the great shepherd of the sheep, by the blood of the eternal covenant, equip you with everything good that you may do his will, working in you that which is pleasing in his sight, through Jesus Christ; to whom be glory for ever and ever. Amen.

Hebrews 13:20-21 RSV

The above list of encouraging passages from God's Word is not exhaustive. Here are some additional verses you may want to read and meditate on: Psalms 27, 46, 62, 130, 146; Isaiah 43:1–3.

Appendix C

Questions for Individual Reflection or Group Discussion

1. Are there any pictures of anxiety hanging on the wall of your memory?

2. How do those memories shape how you deal with worry today?

3. What are the causes of worry in your life today?

4. How are you responding to the commandment to "be anxious for nothing"?

5. How do you know when your concern has morphed into worry and anxiety?

6. In what ways can you address corporate anxiety in your local church?

7. Read 2 Corinthians 12:7–10 and answer the following questions.

   a. Do you think Paul experienced anxiety about his thorn in the flesh?

   b. What specifically was his request? What was God's answer?

   c. What was Paul's response to God's answer?

   d. How can the message of sufficient grace help us when God does not grant our requests?

   e. How does the knowledge that God might have another plan affect your level of anxiety? How should this affect your level of anxiety?

   f. What is Paul's response in the remainder of verse 9 and in verse 10?

8. Can you recall a time when you dared to take God at His word, instead of living by your feelings and internal impressions? Describe your experience.

9. Have you ever experienced God's peace in the context of difficulty? If yes, what did the experience of God's peace look like in your life?

10. God's peace is granted to us through the power and ministry of the Holy Spirit. Are you filled with the Spirit? If not, why not?

11. Read Psalm 119:165 and Isaiah 48:18. What is the connection between obedience to the Lord's Word and the experience of peace?

12. How has your experience of God's peace impacted your witness to others about Christ?

Notes

Chapter 1: The Troubled Waters of Worry

1. Gary R. Collins, *Christian Counseling: A Comprehensive Guide* (Nashville: Thomas Nelson, 2007), 140.

Chapter 2: A Bold Imperative

1. This quotation is often attributed to Dr. Seuss.
2. Gary R. Collins, *Christian Counseling* (Dallas: Word Publishing, 1988), 79.

Chapter 3: The Antidote to Worry

1. J. B. Phillips, *The New Testament in Modern English* (New York: Simon & Schuster, 1958), 230.
2. A. W. Tozer, *The Knowledge of the Holy* (New York: HarperCollins, 1961), 66.
3. Charles Spurgeon, "Prayer Certified of Success" (sermon, Metropolitan Tabernacle, Newington, January 19, 1873), https://www.ccel.org/ccel/spurgeon/sermons19.iii.html.
4. Andrew Murray, *With Christ in the School of Prayer* (New Kensington, PA: Whitaker House, 1981), 41–42.
5. Tozer, *Knowledge of the Holy*, 56.
6. Ibid., 57.
7. Joseph M. Scriven, "What a Friend We Have in Jesus," *Hymns of the Christian Life* (Camp Hill, PA: Christian Publications, 1978), 204.

Chapter 5: Walking in Freedom from Worry

1. J. I. Packer, *Knowing God* (Downers Grove, IL: InterVarsity Press, 1973), 23.
2. A. W. Tozer, *The Knowledge of the Holy* (New York: HarperCollins, 1961), 49.

Acknowledgments

This book grew out of my preaching ministry. After I preached Philippians 4:6–7 at Judson Baptist Church, Dave Schlueter, one of the elders, said to me, "You should develop that sermon into a book. It speaks to the human condition and may be used of the Lord to help people." Dave's words gave me the final push I needed to write the book. Thanks, Dave. I am grateful to the administration of the Moody Bible Institute who granted me sabbatical leave during the fall semester of 2015, during which I wrote the early chapters of the manuscript. I am grateful to Mrs. Jill White, who interacted with my earlier chapters and suggested improvements before I submitted the chapters to a publisher. I am grateful to Moody Publishers for taking on this project. I am grateful to Ingrid Beck, my editor. She worked editorial wonders on my manuscript, providing me with wise editorial guidance and counsel. I am grateful to Connor Sterchi, who walked me through the final editing stages. Finally, I am grateful to the Lord Jesus, the Prince of Peace, who gave me grace, help, strength, and peace as I penned the words of this book. To Him be the glory.